SKOKIE PUBLIC LIBRARY

3 1232 00629 3387

FEB    2012

D1266008

JR. GRAPHIC AMERICAN LEGENDS

# DANIEL BOONE

SKOKIE PUBLIC LIBRARY

Andrea P. Smith

**PowerKiDS**
press

New York

Published in 2012 by The Rosen Publishing Group, Inc.
29 East 21st Street, New York, NY 10010

Copyright © 2012 by The Rosen Publishing Group, Inc.

All rights reserved. No part of this book may be reproduced in any form without permission in writing from the publisher, except by a reviewer.

First Edition

Editor: Joanne Randolph
Book Design: Planman Technologies
Illustrations: Planman Technologies

Library of Congress Cataloging-in-Publication Data

Smith, Andrea P.
  Daniel Boone / by Andrea P. Smith. — 1st ed.
      p. cm. — (Jr. graphic American legends)
  Includes index.
  ISBN 978-1-4488-5194-2 (library binding) — ISBN 978-1-4488-5226-0 (pbk.) — ISBN 978-1-4488-5227-7 (6-pack)
  1. Boone, Daniel, 1734–1820—Juvenile literature. 2. Pioneers—Kentucky—Biography—Juvenile literature. 3. Explorers—Kentucky—Biography—Juvenile literature. 4. Frontier and pioneer life—Kentucky—Juvenile literature. 5. Kentucky—Biography—Juvenile literature. 6. Kentucky—Discovery and exploration—Juvenile literature. 7. Boone, Daniel, 1734–1820—Comic books, strips, etc. 8. Frontier and pioneer life—Kentucky—Comic books, strips, etc. 9. Kentucky—Discovery and exploration—Comic books, strips, etc. 10. Graphic novels. I. Title.
  F454.B66S65 2012
  976.9'02092—dc22
  [B]
                                                              2011001714

Library of Congress Cataloging-in-Publication Data

CPSIA Compliance Information: Batch #PLS1102PK: For Further Information contact Rosen Publishing, New York, New York at 1-800-237-9932

# Contents

# Main Characters

Daniel Boone (1734–1820) Legendary **frontiersman**. He helped **blaze** a trail through the Cumberland Mountains. The trail became known as the Wilderness Road.

Rebecca Bryan (1740–1813) Daniel Boone's wife. She raised ten children with Boone.

John Stuart (?–1769) A **companion** on Boone's first trip through Cumberland Gap. He probably died during the trip.

John Finley (1700s) A frontiersman. He explored Kentucky along the Ohio River fourteen years before Boone.

Jemima Boone (c. 1762–1800s) Boone's daughter. She was **kidnapped** by the **Shawnee** when she was fourteen years old.

# DANIEL BOONE

5

6

THE TRAIL THAT BOONE MADE BECAME KNOWN AS THE WILDERNESS ROAD.

THE MEN BUILT A **STOCKADE** ALONG THE RIVER. SOON SETTLERS MOVED HERE. THEY NAMED THEIR NEW TOWN BOONESBOROUGH AFTER DANIEL BOONE.

JEMIMA AND THE GIRLS LEFT SIGNS ALONG THE TRAIL.

THEY'RE BREAKING THESE BRANCHES ON PURPOSE.

THE GIRLS ARE HELPING US FIND THEM.

DADDY!

I WAS SO SCARED!

YOU FOUND US!

BOONE AND THE OTHER MEN **RESCUED** THE GIRLS.

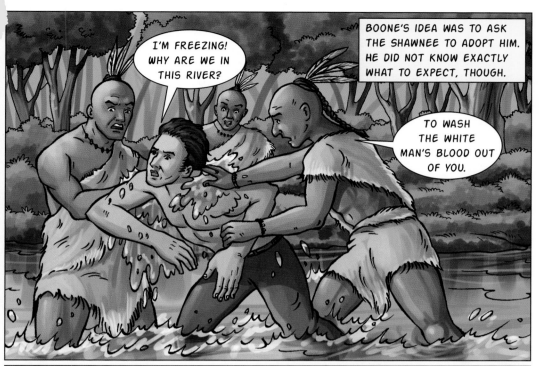

17

BOONE AND REBECCA DID STAY. THEY LIVED THE REST OF THEIR LIVES ON A BIG PLOT OF LAND IN MISSOURI.

IN 1784, JOHN FILSON WROTE A BOOK ABOUT KENTUCKY. HE INCLUDED A **BIOGRAPHY** OF THE LEGENDARY FRONTIERSMAN, DANIEL BOONE.

THEN IN THE 1820S, JAMES FENIMORE COOPER WROTE ABOUT A MAN NAMED NATTY BUMPPO.

# Timeline

| | |
|---|---|
| **November 2, 1734** | Daniel Boone is born in Berks County, Pennsylvania. |
| **1750** | The Boone family moves to North Carolina. |
| **August 14, 1756** | Daniel Boone marries Rebecca Bryan. |
| **1765** | Daniel Boone travels to Florida with some friends to explore the area. |
| **1767** | Daniel Boone goes to Kentucky twice to hunt, trap, and explore the region. |
| **1768** | John Finley asks Daniel Boone to find a gap through the Cumberland Mountains from North Carolina and Virginia into Kentucky. |
| **Spring 1775** | Daniel Boone blazes the Wilderness Road through the Cumberland Mountains. He forms a settlement named Boonesborough along the Kentucky River. |
| **Fall 1775** | Daniel Boone moves his family from North Carolina to Boonesborough. |
| **July 1776** | Daniel Boone's daughter, Jemima Boone, is kidnapped by Shawnee warriors. |
| **February 1778** | Daniel Boone is kidnapped by the Shawnee and adopted. |
| **October 1779** | Twenty thousand pioneers settle in Boonesborough. |
| **1784** | John Filson publishes a book about Kentucky, which includes a biography of Daniel Boone. |
| **June 1, 1792** | Kentucky becomes the fifteenth state. |
| **1799** | Daniel Boone moves his family to St. Louis, Missouri. |
| **1803** | The United States buys the Louisiana territory from France in the Louisiana Purchase. |
| **1820** | Daniel Boone dies at 85 years of age. |

# Glossary

**biography** (by-AH-gruh-fee)  Book that gives a history of a person's life.

**blaze** (BLAYZ)  Make a mark on a tree or rock to show a trail.

**companion** (com-PAN-yun)  A friend or a pal.

**frontiersman** (frun-TEERZ-mun)  A person who lives and works in an area that has not yet been settled.

**gap** (GAP)  A pass, or opening, through the mountains.

**homey** (HOM-ee)  Comfortable or homelike.

**kidnapped** (KID-napt)  Carried off a person by force.

**legend** (LEH-jend)  A story, passed down through the years, that cannot be proved.

**rescued** (RES-kyood)  Saved someone or something from danger.

**replica** (REH-plih-kuh)  A copy.

**restless** (RES-less)  Uncomfortable staying in one spot, wanting to move around.

**Shawnee** (shah-NEE)  Native Americans who lived in the Ohio Valley, which includes Kentucky.

**stockade** (stah-KAYD)  A wooden wall made of large, strong posts. The posts are put upright in the ground to help protect the area inside the wall.

**swamp** (SWOMP)  A wet land with a lot of trees and bushes.

**tracking** (TRAK-ing)  Following a trail.

**wilderness** (WIL-dur-nis)  An area that has no lasting settlements.

# Index

# Web Sites

Due to the changing nature of Internet links, Power Kids Press has developed an online list of Web sites related to the subject of this book. This site is updated regularly. Please use this link to access the list:

www.powerkidslinks.com/JGAM/boone